WHAT CAN I SEE?

CORAL REEF

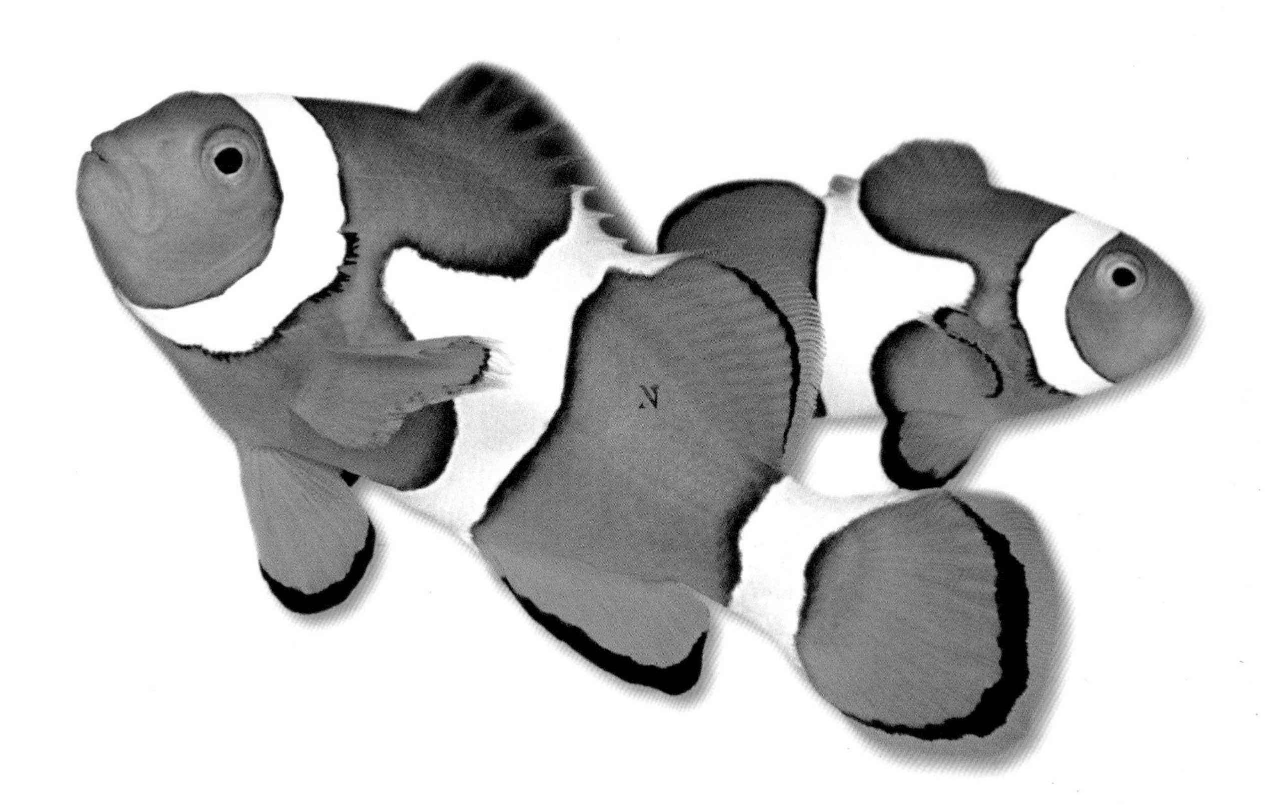

ticktock

First published in Great Britain in 2006 by ticktock Media Ltd.,
Unit 2, Orchard Business Centre, North Farm Road, Tunbridge Wells, Kent TN2 3XF

ISBN 1 86007 853 2
Printed in China

Picture credits

t=top, b=bottom, c=centre, l=left, r=right
Corbis: 3b, 13c. NHPA: 11tr. Alamy: 6cl. FLPA: 4-5, 9c, 10c, 18-19c, 21c, 23c, 24tr.
Every effort has been made to trace the copyright holders, and we apologise in advance for any unintentional omissions. We would be pleased to insert the appropriate acknowledgements in any subsequent edition of this publication.

A CIP catalogue record for this book is available from the British Library.

contents

On a coral reef

There is so much to see on a coral reef, from fabulous fish darting between the corals to larger animals that **lumber** along the bottom.

What can you see on a coral reef?

Lobster

Shark

Sea snake

Sponge

Jellyfish

Turtle

Clown fish

Lion fish

Sea anemone

Lobster

Lobsters are strange-looking creatures that live at the bottom of the ocean. They have soft bodies which are **protected** by a hard shell.

A lobster's eyes are at the end of long **stalks**.

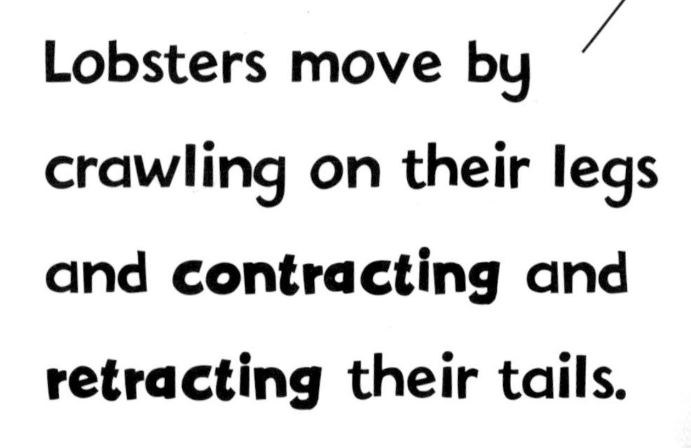

Lobsters move by crawling on their legs and **contracting** and **retracting** their tails.

A lobster has five pairs of legs. Its front legs are much bigger than the rest of its legs.

Pincers act a bit like a finger and thumb. They help the lobster to hold on to its **prey**.

Shark

A shark is a kind of fish with a long body and very sharp teeth. The most dangerous kind is the Great White Shark.

Shark use their teeth to attack their prey. They are sharp enough to tear **flesh** easily.

Sharks' eyes are much more **sensitive** to light than human eyes, making hunting at night easy.

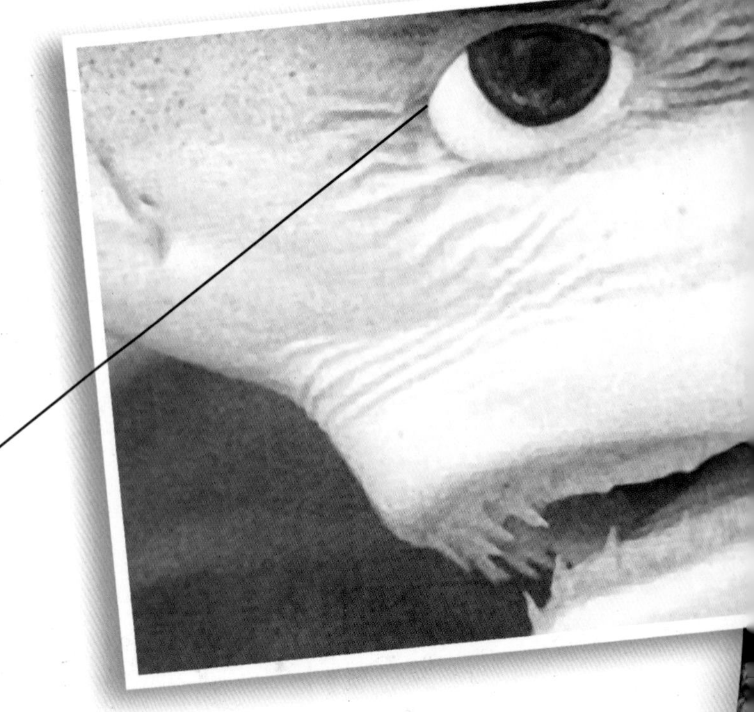

A shark's bullet-shaped body allows it to cut easily through water. It uses its fins for **steering** and balance.

sea snake

Sea snakes live in **shallow** water and come up to the surface to breathe air. They have **nostrils** which close up when they are under the water.

There are over 50 different kinds of sea snake, and all of them are **poisonous**.

Sea snakes are good swimmers. The ends of their tails are flat like **paddles** to help them swim.

Sea snakes have short **fangs** that **inject** poison into their prey. They can open their mouths wide enough to bite a man's leg.

sponge

Sponges can be found on the bottom of the sea. They look a lot like plants, but they are actually a very simple form of animal.

Real sponges are collected and sold for people to use.

The surface of a sponge is covered with holes called ostia. These suck in the tiny ocean creatures that the sponge eats.

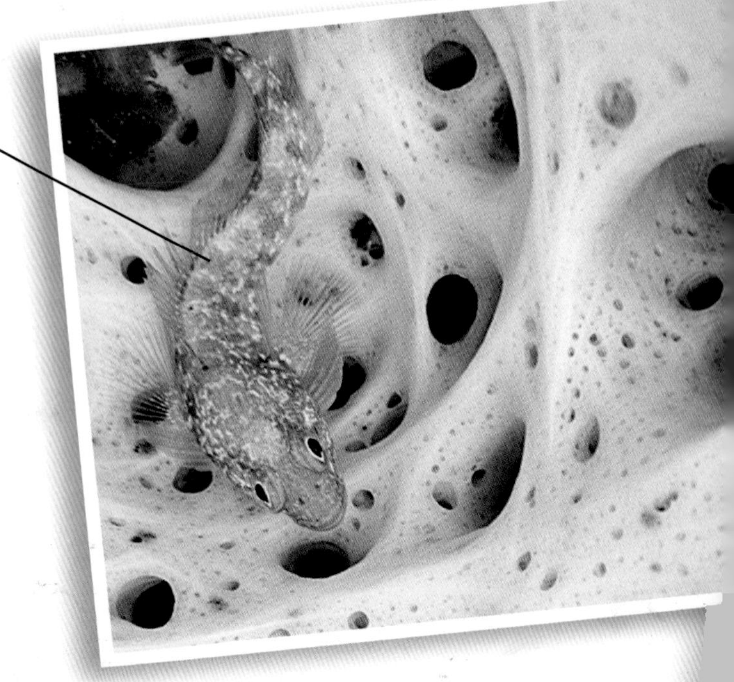

Sponges ***attach*** themselves to something hard and never move again.

Jellyfish

There are many different kinds of jellyfish. The smallest is just a few centimetres across, but the largest can be more than a metre across.

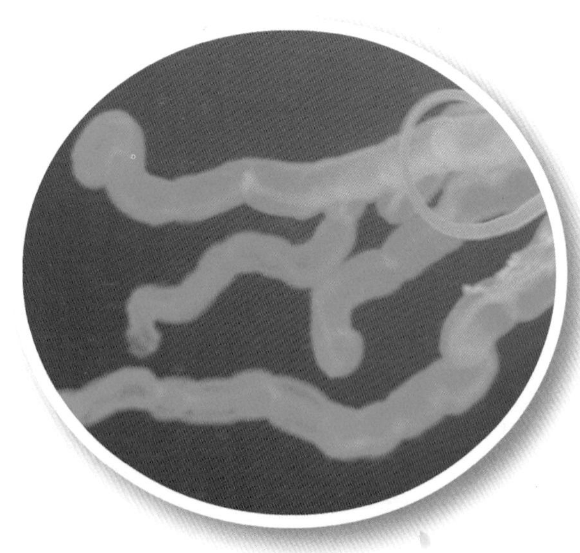

Jellyfish have long, stinging **tentacles**. They sting if they touch another animal.

A jellyfish's mouth is under its body. As well as tentacles, it has **oral** arms which it uses to put food into its mouth.

Around 80 per cent of a jellyfish's body is water.

turtle

Turtles are found in oceans all over the world. The largest kind can weigh more than 500 kilogrammes.

The turtle has a hard shell which protects its soft body.

A turtle has strong **flippers** instead of legs. It can swim well, but it can only walk very slowly on land.

Turtles come on to land to **bask** in the sun, sleep and lay their eggs.

Turtles lay their eggs in sand. They dig holes using their front flippers and bury them. A female turtle can lay up to 100 eggs.

clownfish

These tiny fish have a very strange friendship with sea anemones. They live in warm oceans wherever sea anemones are found.

The name clown fish comes from the bright markings which look like clown make-up.

The bright markings **attract** other creatures for the sea anemone to eat.

Clown fish are protected from an anemone's sting by a coating called **mucus.**

Clown fish usually live in pairs. They lay their eggs on rocks next to the sea anemone.

Lion fish

Lion fish have striped bodies and **poisonous** spines all around their bodies. They live in holes and caves in the reef and come out at night to hunt for food.

Lionfish prefer to live alone or in family groups.

The poisonous spines of the lion fish help to protect it from **predators**.

Lion fish usually swim slowly,
but they can swim fast
when they attack.

sea anemone

The sea anemone looks like a flower, but it is an animal. It spends its life attached to the ocean floor and can grow to a height of 1.8 metres.

There are many different kinds of sea anemone. Some are very colourful.

The body of a sea anemone is shaped like a column. Its mouth is at the top.

Clown fish help the sea anemone by attracting other ocean creatures for it to eat. The clown fish eats what is left.

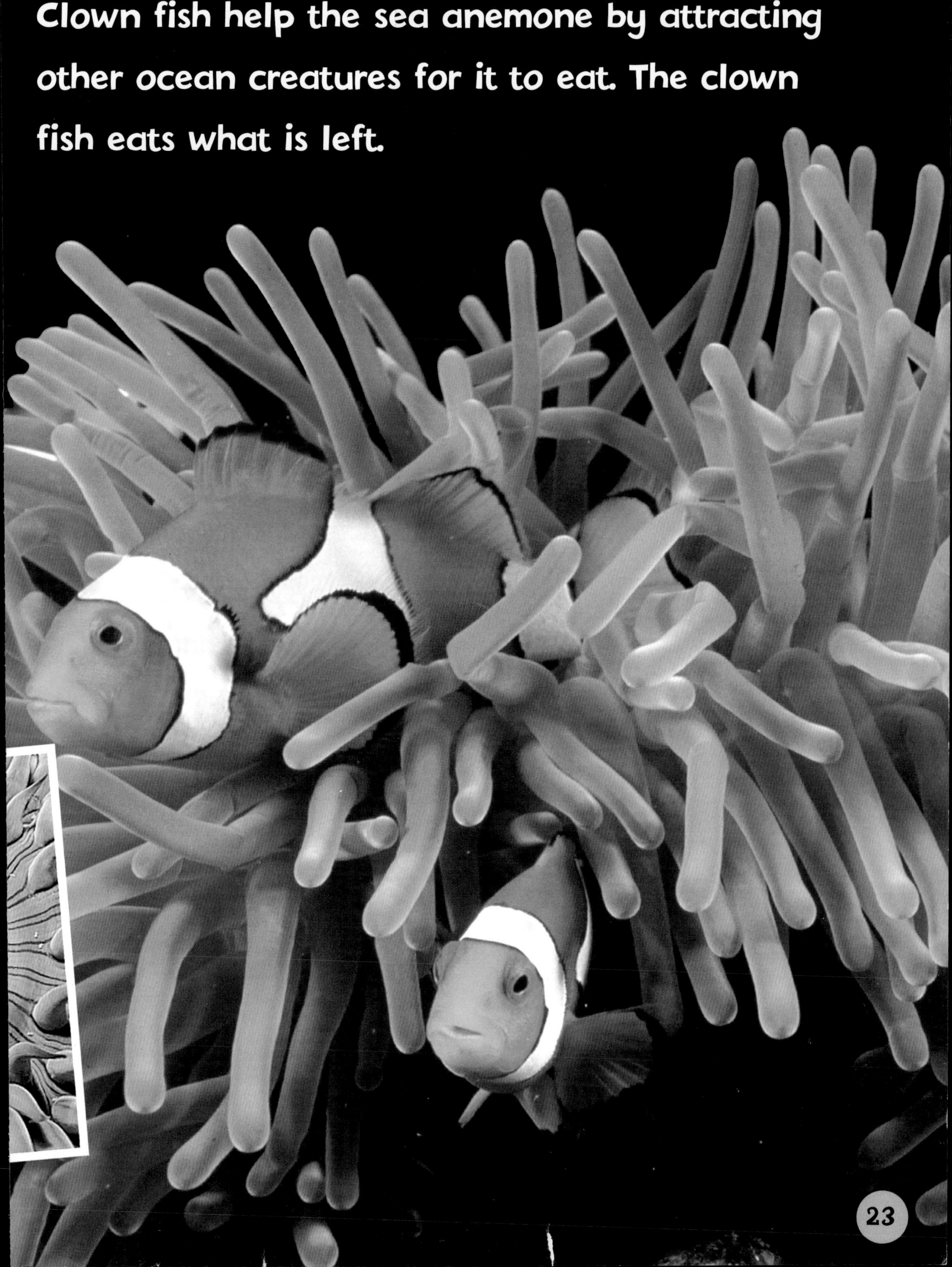

Glossary

Attach Join on or fix to

Attract Make other creatures come near by looking good or interesting

Bask Lie in the warmth of the sun

Bolumn A tall shape, like a pole

Contracting To get smaller by drawing together

Fangs Hollow teeth used to bite and squirt out poison

Flesh The soft part of the body of an animal or human being

Flippers Flat arm-like growths that help with swimming

Inject Squirt or push out

Lumber To move along very slowly

Mucus A slimy substance which coats animals as protection

Nostrils The holes that animals and humans breathe through

Oral To do with the mouth

Paddle An oar with a flat end

Pincer A kind of claw with two parts that can move in and out.

Poisonous Capable of harming or killing by poison

Predator An animal that hunts and eats other animals

Prey An animal that is caught and eaten by another animal

Protect Keep safe, look after

Retracting To draw back

Sensitive Able to sense things

Shallow Not very deep

Stalk A long, thin structure

Steering To guide something

Tentacles Long arm-like growths